walk with me.

a grandfather's story

a guided journal of memories
for my grandchild

Other Books In The "Walk With Me" Series:

A Great-Grandmother's Story
A Great-Grandfather's Story
A Grandmother's Story
A Mother's Story
A Father's Story
A Stepmother's Story
A Stepfather's Story
A Sister's Story

wandering tortoise

ISBN: 978-1796846775

Introduction

This guided journal is a fantastic way to create
a one-of-a-kind keepsake for your grandchild!
You can choose to complete one page a day
or several at once.
Pages can be completed in any order you desire.

Includes 112 thought-provoking writing prompts
written from the perspective of your grandchild.
Write as though you are speaking directly to them.

Also includes:
A Five-Generation Family Tree
Two Recipe Pages
Two Dot Grid Pages For Drawing Diagrams
(floor plans, property boundaries, room layout, etc.)

There are plenty of places for writing,
but there are also empty pages at the beginning
and end of each section that can be filled with
photographs, clippings, and anything else you wish
to include to help bring your stories to life.

_____

Your Full Name

_____

Your Date of Birth

_____

Your Place of Birth

_____

the date you began this journal

_____

the person you are completing this journal for

Family

Our

Your Paternal Grandfather

_____

B: _____ D: _____

M: _____

Your Paternal Grandmother

_____

B: _____ D: _____

Your Maternal Grandfather

_____

B: _____ D: _____

M: _____

Your Maternal Grandmother

_____

B: _____ D: _____

Your Father

_____

B: _____ D: _____

M: _____

Your Mother

_____

B: _____ D: _____

B = Born
M = Married
D = Died

Family Tree

You

B: _____

My Grandmother

B: _____

M: _____

My Parent (your child)

B: _____

My Parent

B: _____

M: _____

Me (your grandchild)

B: _____

Where did your name come from?
Does it have special meaning?
Were you named after a family member?

Did you have a nickname that everyone called you?
How did you get that nickname?
What do family members call you now?

Describe your mother.
What is your favorite memory
of your mother?

Describe your father.
What is your favorite memory
of your father?

Do you feel you more closely resemble
your mother or your father?
In what way?

Were you able to see your grandparents often when you were young?
Where did they live? What were they like?

Did your grandparents ever tell stories about their past?
What did you learn about them?

Did you know your great-grandparents?
Describe them.

Were you the oldest child, the middle child, the youngest child or the only child in your family? How do you feel this has influenced your life?

Tell about any brothers or sisters you had. Did you usually get along with them?

How did your family
spend quality time together?

_____

_____

_____

_____

_____

_____

_____

_____

_____

_____

_____

_____

_____

_____

_____

_____

_____

_____

_____

What do you feel was the most important lesson your parents taught you?

Childhood

What is your earliest memory?

Describe your childhood home.
If you had more than one, describe your favorite.
Was it small or large? In a rural area or urban?

Draw a layout of your childhood home or yard.

Describe what a typical day was like in your childhood home.

What occupations did your parents or guardians have? Did you see them often or were they frequently away?

What types of chores were you expected to do? Was there a chore that you especially liked or disliked?

_____

_____

_____

_____

_____

_____

_____

_____

_____

_____

_____

_____

_____

_____

_____

_____

_____

_____

_____

_____

_____

Did you get an allowance?
How much was it?
What did you typically spend it on?

Do you have a favorite holiday tradition from your childhood?
What is it, and why is it your favorite?

What was your favorite childhood toy or activity?

Did you have any childhood illnesses or diseases or any notable medical emergencies?

_____

_____

_____

_____

_____

_____

_____

_____

_____

_____

_____

_____

_____

_____

_____

_____

_____

_____

_____

As a child, what did you want to be
when you grew up?
Was there anything that influenced this decision?

Did you have a favorite bedtime story when you were a child? Did you tell that same story to your own children when they were young?

Is there a frightening memory from childhood that you still remember vividly today?

What was your favorite meal growing up?
Did a particular person make it or did it come from a special restaurant? Do you still enjoy it today?

If you know the recipe, please share it.

Recipe: _____

# of Servings: _____

Ingredients:

_____   _____

_____   _____

_____   _____

_____   _____

_____   _____

_____   _____

Instructions:

_____

_____

_____

_____

_____

_____

_____

_____

_____

Did you have an idol or hero as a child?
Why was this particular person
your favorite?

Who or what do you remember most fondly from your childhood?

_____

_____

_____

_____

_____

_____

_____

_____

_____

_____

_____

_____

_____

_____

_____

_____

_____

_____

_____

_____

Teenage Years

What school did you attend during your teenage years? Did you enjoy school? Would you have preferred a different school?

What was your school dress code?
Describe what you would typically wear to school.

Did you participate in school sports, clubs or other school activities?

Describe your typical school day.

What was your favorite school subject?
Who was your favorite teacher? Why?

What school subject did you find the easiest?
What subject was the most challenging for you?

Did you participate in a youth group or youth organization? How has this experience influenced your adult life?

What trends or fads were popular when you were young?
Did you participate in those fads?

_____

_____

_____

_____

_____

_____

_____

_____

_____

_____

_____

_____

_____

_____

_____

_____

_____

_____

_____

What did you and your friends like to do for fun? Did you have a favorite hangout?

Did you have a best friend?
What was their name?
What do you remember most about them?

Did you ever get into trouble as a teenager? What kinds of consequences would you face?

How old were you when you started dating?
Where did you typically go on dates?

Did you have a curfew? What time was it? What would happen if you ever missed curfew?

Did you have a job when you were a teenager? What was it? How much were you paid? What responsibilities did you have?

At any time during your youth, did you save your money for something special? What was it? How did you earn the money for it?

When you were a teenager, what did you think you wanted to do when you became an adult? What influenced your decision?

Adulthood

Did you receive any education or training beyond high school? What was it?
Did you earn any degrees or certifications?

What jobs have you had in your adult life?

How did you choose your career path?

What was your favorite job? How much did the job pay? Why was it your favorite?

When did you get your first car?
What make and model was it?
How did having a car change your lifestyle?

Did you serve in the military?
If so, in what branch of service? For how long?
What was your rank when you left service?

What is your most memorable moment, from your time in the military?

What organizations or groups have you belonged to as an adult? How did you become involved in them?

Love & Marriage

When and how did you meet
my grandmother?
What was it about her that attracted you?

Describe your first date with my grandmother.

_____

_____

_____

_____

_____

_____

_____

_____

_____

_____

_____

_____

_____

_____

_____

_____

_____

_____

What is your favorite memory about my grandmother?

What did your parents think about my grandmother when you first introduced them?

Describe your wedding ceremony.
Who was there to celebrate with you?

Did you have a honeymoon?
If so, where did you go and
what do you remember most about the place?

Describe the first house or apartment you shared with each other. What did you do to make it a home?

Draw a layout of the first home you shared.

Were you married more than once? How do you feel your marriage to my grandmother differed from your other marriage(s)?

Parenting

How did you feel when you found out you were going to be a father?

Tell me about your children.
How many have you had? Describe them.

How did you choose names for your child/children?
Are they named after special people in your life?

Tell about the day
my mother/father was born.

How did you feel when your children started school? Were you excited? Nervous? Scared?

Do you feel you were
a strict parent or a lenient parent?

Was your parenting style similar to the way you were raised or was it different? Was that by choice or circumstance?

What do you feel was the most difficult part of raising a child?

What was your scariest moment
as a parent?

Describe a rewarding moment in your life as a parent.

If you could turn back time, would you choose to raise your family differently? If so, what would you change?

Is there a family favorite recipe you make?
Where did it come from?
How did it become your specialty?

_____

_____

_____

_____

_____

_____

_____

_____

_____

_____

_____

_____

_____

_____

_____

_____

_____

_____

_____

_____

_____

Please share your special recipe.

Recipe: _____

# of Servings: _____

Ingredients:

_____ _____

_____ _____

_____ _____

_____ _____

_____ _____

_____

Instructions:

_____

_____

_____

_____

_____

_____

_____

_____

How did you feel when you found out you were going to be a grandfather?

_____
_____
_____
_____
_____
_____
_____
_____
_____
_____
_____
_____
_____
_____
_____
_____
_____
_____
_____

Did you give my mother/father any advice about parenting? What was your advice?

_____

_____

_____

_____

_____

_____

_____

_____

_____

_____

_____

_____

_____

_____

_____

_____

_____

_____

What is your favorite thing about being a grandfather?

More About You

How would you describe yourself?
Creative? Funny? Logical?
Handy? Generous? Spontaneous?

_____

_____

_____

_____

_____

_____

_____

_____

_____

_____

_____

_____

_____

_____

_____

_____

_____

Is there anything about yourself that you would change if you could? What is it and why?

What hobbies do you have?
How or why did you start this hobby?

Do you know how to play a musical instrument? How long have you played it? Is there an instrument you would like to learn how to play?

Have you ever received any special awards or recognitions in your life?
What were they, and when did you receive them?

Do you practice a religion?
Is it the same religion as
your parents and grandparents?

How do you feel religion has influenced your life?

What is your favorite holiday?
What is your favorite thing about it?

Who is your best friend now?
How long have you known them?
What draws you to them?

_____

_____

_____

_____

_____

_____

_____

_____

_____

_____

_____

_____

_____

_____

_____

_____

_____

_____

What are your "good habits"?
Do you have any "bad habits"?

Describe an occasion
when you were proud of yourself.

Favorites

Food: _____

Cuisine: _____

Dessert: _____

Drink: _____

Candy: _____

Game or Sport: _____

Athlete: _____

Book: _____

Author: _____

Television Show: _____

Movie: _____

Movie Genre: _____

Actor or Actress: _____

Composer: _____

Song: _____

Singer: _____

Music Genre: _____

Animal: _____

Vacation Destination: _____

Thing You Can't Live Without: _____

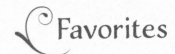
Favorites

Pastime: _____

Modern Convenience: _____

Place to Shop: _____

Gadget or Tool: _____

Flower: _____

Person in History: _____

House Style: _____

Color: _____

Artist: _____

Article of Clothing: _____

Motivational Speaker: _____

Type of Weather: _____

Way to Relax : _____

Warm Weather Activity: _____

Cold Weather Activity: _____

Season: _____

Holiday: _____

Quote or Verse: _____

Thing to Collect: _____

Car: _____

Looking Back

What has been your favorite age or stage in life so far? Why?

What is something you used a lot in your past that has been replaced by a modern substitute? Which do you prefer? Why?

What is the first movie
you remember seeing in a theater?
How have movie theaters changed since then?

What was your initial reaction to home computers?
How do you feel about them now?

What was your initial reaction to the internet? Has your view changed over time? Do you use the internet for shopping, research or socializing?

How many pets have you had?
Describe your favorite pet.

Tell about a compliment you have received that has had an impact on your life. Who gave you that compliment?

Describe a difficult choice
that you have had to make in your life.
How did you reach your decision?

Name one person you wish you could see again. What would you say or do when you saw them.

Have you traveled much?
What places have you been?
What has been your favorite place to visit?

What is your favorite vacation memory, either from your childhood or from a trip taken more recently?

What is the best advice that you have received?
Who gave you that advice?

Regarding world events and politics, how do you feel the views of your parents and grandparents have influenced your own perspective?

What social issues of today did you see during your childhood?
Do you feel things have improved?

What are the most significant differences you see between the world of your childhood and the world at present?

What hardships have you experienced in your life?
What challenges did you face?
How did you overcome those challenges?

What is something you feel you would do differently if given the chance? What impact do you feel this change would have on your life?

What are some defining moments in your life?

What wars have been fought in your lifetime?
How do you feel they have impacted your life?

Do you have any unfulfilled dreams? Something you have always wanted to do but haven't?

Do you have any disappointments or regrets? Tell me about them.

Looking Forward

What skills or special knowledge do you have that you would like to pass down to the next generation?

What are some new skills
you would like to learn?

What goals or dreams
are you working toward right now?

What do you want your children and grandchildren to learn from your life?

What family traditions do you hope your children and grandchildren carry on?

_____

_____

_____

_____

_____

_____

_____

_____

_____

_____

_____

_____

_____

_____

_____

_____

_____

_____

What advice would you like to share with your family and friends?